ROCK

BookLife

Written by
Harriet Brundle

©2017
Book Life
King's Lynn
Norfolk PE30 4LS

ISBN: 978-1-786370-36-5

Written by:
Harriet Brundle

Edited by:
Grace Jones

Designed by:
Danielle Jones

A catalogue record for this book
is available from the British Library.

Contents

The orange words in this book can be found in the glossary on page 23.

What is a Material?

Materials are what things are made of. Some materials are natural and some are man-made.

Water

Rock

Wood

Glass

Plastic

Metal

Every material has its own properties. A material might be very soft. This would be one of its properties.

Pyjamas, cuddly toys and pillows are all soft.

What is Rock?

Rock is a natural material that is found all over Earth. The layer of rock covering the Earth's surface is called the crust. Rock is a solid material.

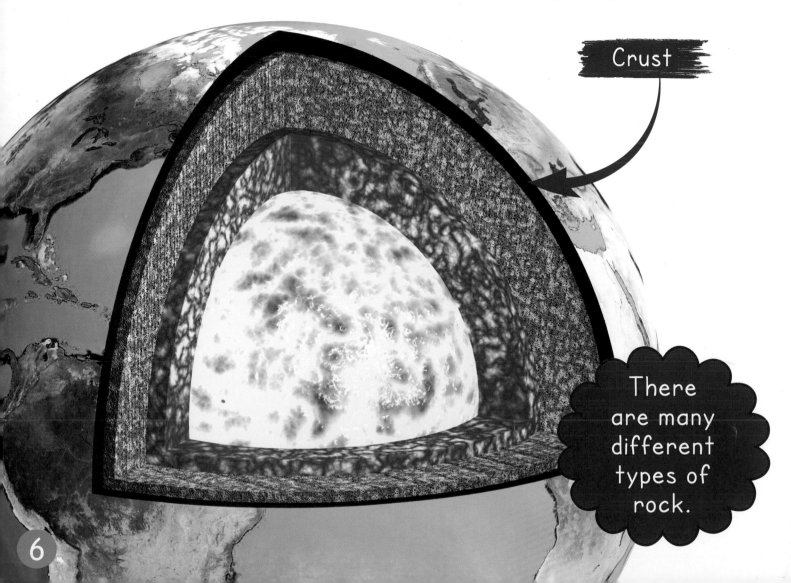

Crust

There are many different types of rock.

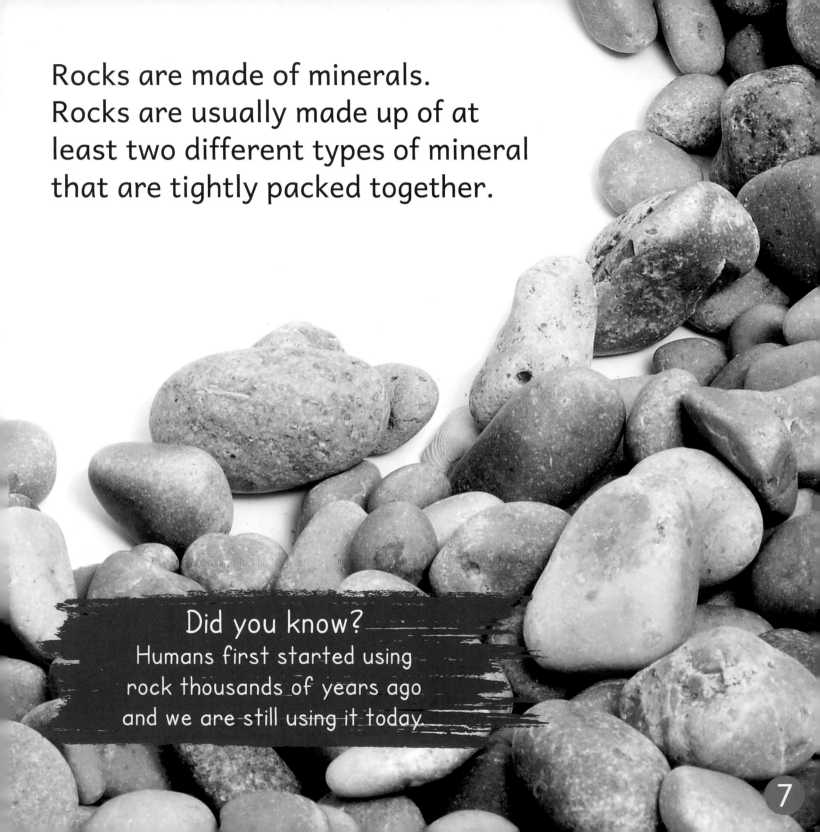

Rocks are made of minerals.
Rocks are usually made up of at
least two different types of mineral
that are tightly packed together.

Did you know?
Humans first started using
rock thousands of years ago
and we are still using it today

Types of Rock

Rocks are organised into three main groups: igneous, sedimentary and metamorphic. All rocks can be put into one of these three groups based on their properties.

Metamorphic

Igneous

Sedimentary

Igneous rocks are made when hot magma cools.
You can usually see crystals inside igneous rocks.

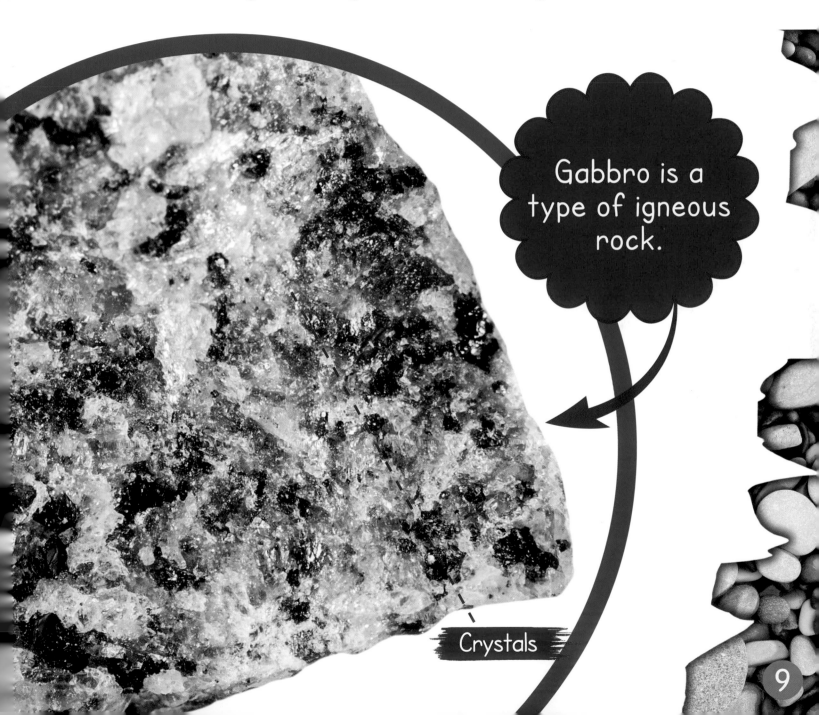

Gabbro is a type of igneous rock.

Crystals

Sedimentary rocks are made when pieces of sediment are pressed together over a long period of time. Limestone is a sedimentary rock.

This type of rock will usually have many different layers.

Metamorphic rocks are formed when rocks are put under very high heat and pressure.

Lapis lazuli is a type of metamorphic rock. It is often used to make jewellery.

Lapis Lazuli

Scientists can identify different types of rock by how hard they are and by the way they look. Rocks can be different colours, have layers or holes or they might even be reflective.

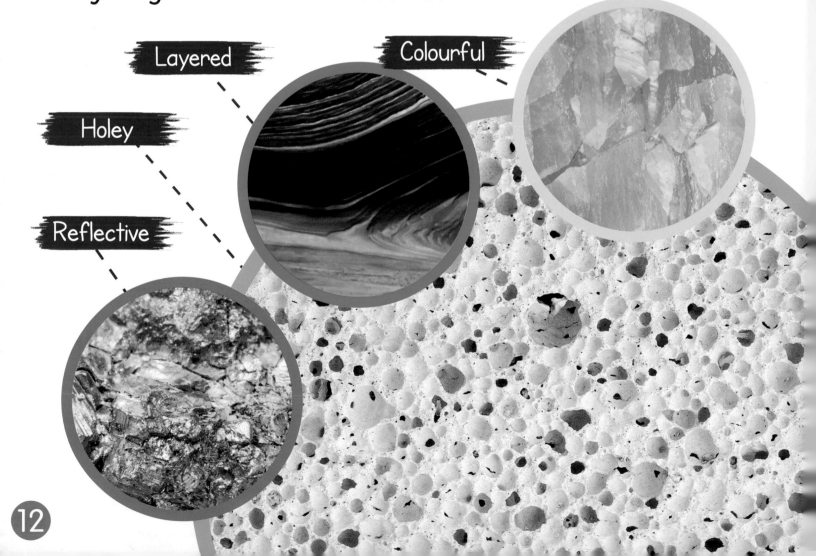

Layered

Colourful

Holey

Reflective

Slate is impermeable, which means that water cannot go through it. Slate is often used to make roof tiles because it stops rain water from getting into buildings.

Chalk is a crumbly rock that can be easily broken.

Slate

We use some types of rock in our homes. Granite is often used to make kitchen worktops because it is hard, strong and durable.

Granite

Limestone can be used to build houses.

14

Pumice is used in health products such as soap and foot scrubs. Marble is very strong, so it is often used to make floors and statues.

Coal is a type of rock that can be burnt to give off heat and produce energy.

Rock in Heat

It takes a temperature of between 600 and 1,300 degrees Celsius to melt rock. When a rock melts, it turns into lava.

Lava

Celsius is a measure of temperature.

The high temperatures needed to melt rock are usually only found inside the core of planet Earth.

Rocks are pushed downwards as the Earth's crust moves. As the rocks are pushed deeper into the Earth, the temperature gets hotter and hotter until the rocks melt.

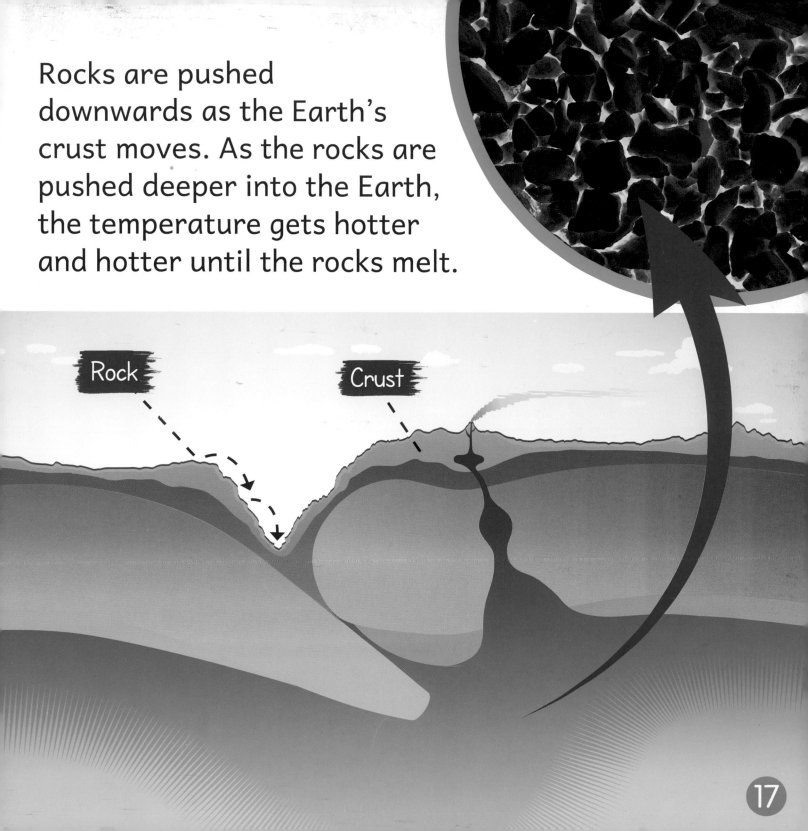

Rock

Crust

Rocks Around the World

The Rock of Gibraltar, near Spain, is made out of limestone and is thought to be around 200 million years old!

There are over 200 monkeys living on the rock.

The Black Stone of Mecca, in the country of Saudi Arabia, is a very special place for Muslims. The large, dark coloured rock has been rubbed smooth from many hands touching it.

Precious Stones

Precious stones are rocks or minerals that are used in jewellery or are collected. Precious stones are usually more expensive to buy than other types of rock.

Some types of precious stone include diamonds, rubies, emeralds and sapphires.

Ruby

Emerald

Sapphire

Diamonds are extremely hard. The only thing that can scratch a diamond is another diamond.

21

Activities

With an adult, go outside and collect 10 different rocks. Look at and touch each rock that you have found.

Is it rough or smooth?

What colour is it?

Is it big or small?

Do you notice anything else about the rock?

Do any of the rocks you have found look like they might be igneous, sedimentary or metamorphic rocks?

Glossary

Core
the middle of something.

Crystals
clear and often colourful types of rock that sometimes have a very beautiful appearance.

Durable
able to last a long time without being damaged.

Magma
hot, liquid rock below or within the Earth's crust.

Man-made
something that is made or caused by humans.

Natural
something that has been made by nature.

Pressure
the force created when something is pressing against something else.

Properties
the different qualities of a material.

Reflective
something that sends back the light that shines on it.

Sediment
small pieces of a solid material, for example sand, that can form a layer of rock.

Index

Photocredits: Abbreviations: l-left, r-right, b-bottom, t-top, c-centre, m-middle.
Front cover top – russ witherington middle – Rodrigo Bellizzi bottom – StrelaStudio. 2 – Fotosr52. 3 – Vaclav Volrab. 4m – Igor Bulgarin 4tl – YanLev 4bl – 3445128471 4bm – Temych 4br – Pressmaster 4tl – Sunny Studio. 5l – wavebreakmedia. 5r – hartphotography. 6 – Lukiyanova Natalia / frent. 7 – nito. 8r – OlegSam 8m – Kashin 8l – Tyler Boyes. 9 – vvoe. 10l– Leene. 11l – Alex Kuzovev 11br – Oliver Mohr. 12tr – Mavrick 12br – Dja65 12m – tonDone 12l – vvoe . 13l – Monkey Business Images. 13r – Robyn Mackenzie. 14l – JuneJ. 14r– Martin Fowler. 15br – Robert Przybysz 15tr – ollirg 15tl – Allen McDavid Stoddard. 16 – www.sandatlas.org. 17b – daulon 17t –. Hollygraphic. 18bm – Sorin Colac 18tr – Natalia Paklina. 19 –Zurijeta. 20 – Pidgorna Ievgeniia. 21 – J. Palys 21b – Atiketta Sangasaeng. 22tr – Lopris 22b – YamabikaY. 24 – valzan.
Images are courtesy of Shutterstock.com. With thanks to Getty Images, Thinkstock Photo and iStockphoto.